A Vicarious Sustenance

A Gentle Ocean of Clashing Waves

Kay Strayed

BookLeaf Publishing

India | USA | UK

Made with ❤ on the BookLeaf Publishing Platform
www.bookleafpub.in
www.bookleafpub.com

Dedication

To the misfits—those
Who are excluded quietly,
Who suffer the subtle itch of wanting to belong—
I see you.
I hear you.
I witness your being.
I am you.
And,
I love you.

Preface

Dawn is such that it imitates nearness—how quiet claims the cold, fresh sea, and night—lonely—turns peaceful. A cheery sense of solace engulfs you in cozy waves of sunlight, the sun blessing you with warmth and a repaired soul for a new day, urging past the dread. So comes the eve of the next breath, the next step—and somehow the quiet claims us for yet another day; another beginning anew.

Writing this book was as much a daunting task as it was a celebration of every encounter, every emotion, every feeling, every breath, and every battle—won or lost—that I have lived. These poems are not one continuous journey but many—almost anthological though not quite.

Do not run through them. Sit with them. Let them breathe alongside you as you walk each line, each word —deliberately chosen to reflect and relay to you my dissonant mind. Let this ocean of words take you to wherever you need and want to be, as it did to me while writing it. I hope you lose and find yourself, again and again, as the waves caress you.

Love, Kay

Acknowledgements

This collection couldn't exist without the world around me. The amalgamation of all my life experiences brought me here—with help from social media algorithms and intense, raw emotions.

I hold eternal gratitude for my younger sibling, Titli, for tolerating me, and growing with me every step of the way. To my therapist, Jayati, who makes living possible for me—and so, so many—thank you for giving me company through the rollercoasters of my pain, elation, and everything in between. To the friends who let me crash at their places when I needed to run away, or run towards something—I am indebted to you, now and forever. Anjali, thank you for the most compassionate stay and a magical visit to the park. The biggest hugs to Aditi and her cat family, for making me feel at home from so far away. Thank you for working with me to maintain such a healthy dynamic of love, warmth, and friendship.

I would like to honour my past selves, my abandoned childhood, my brokenness, and the younger me who always hoped for a better everything. To the parts of me that lay ignored and bereft—consider my grief for you; I cherish you. You all will always be a part of me. May we grow and heal together.

A heartfelt thank you to:
Those who came and left me for the worse,
Those who came and left me for the better,
Those who stayed,
Those I welcomed and those who welcomed me,
Those who showered me with acceptance,
Those who made space for me,
Those I love with all my heart,
Those who call me Kay.

To the heroes that affirm people like me—making room for us in their hearts—and to you:
You breathe life into me.
Take solace, for you are not alone, and never will be.

Delusions

Somewhere past the horizon,
There is a house made of stars.
And it shines bright
On a land of clouds,
With a sky full of grass—
As green as it will ever be,
With raindrops of dirt
Drenching us wet with dry.

This—this is a place
Where the moon shines bright
And the sun lags behind.
This is a place beyond heaven and earth,
This is a place beyond time.

There is a place
Past the horizons,
Invisible to the naked eye—
Too pure for us humans, insatiable
For we bring ruins
To the home that lends us
Breath-full air and thirsty water,
Through wars—lethal, damaging.

Brazen and misanthropic,
I ask—all but love:
Do we not deserve
An affair, an escapade—
The most beautiful sight
Of this garden divine?

Discomfort

If I grant you my seal of approval,
Will you do it? Will you trust me?
Will you:
 Use that product?
 Buy that shirt?
 Try that drink?
 Eat that dessert?
Would you trust me enough
To leap into the uncertain
And dive, a being faithful?

If you took a bullet for me,
If you jumped off that cliff,
Would you blame me?
Would contempt become you?
When the bullet aches,
When you won't see a tomorrow,
Would you be nothing
But curses and loathing?

Will you forgive me instead?
Console me, praise my virtues?
Will you care still—
Would you still love me

If I transgress?
When you no longer recognize me,
Benefit of the doubt will I get?
Absolve me from sin, would you?
Would you accompany me
Downwards, in the heated frenzy—
Or will I be an abandoned soul,
Deserving of my seat in this hell?

Do I deserve a saviour?
Will you worry for me,
Say that I've healed?
What if I repent—
Will you still love me,
The person I've become,
Scars and mistakes all?
Take me as I am?
Would you still trust me?
How would your faith deem me?

Green to Red to Gray

Where do I find my home
In this urban jungle,
Where the horizon itself
Hides behind brick and mortar?

I stay here on the roof,
Watching the day turn dark,
And accept the night's arrival.
The gradients of the sky
Closing in on me—
Planets and stars visible already,
Though not much to count.

How I miss the musings of nature—
The branches, the leaves, the birds,
The night's river of stars,
The life and only life.

We sold our humane
The day we fired our mother
And burned it down to ashes,
To build a new world:
One without sunlit canopies,
One without horizons,

One without life—
A world without soul.

My Body, Her Lineage— Graves Untold

I carry the weight of my world in my breasts
The male gaze in my waist
My character between my legs
Subordination in my tongue
Domesticity in my limbs
I carry the weight of my gender—
Women, one and all
I carry those that came before me
And those I must birth

I carry shame in my eyes
Regret in my breath
Pain in my tears
And all I hold back

I carry burdens on my shoulders
Ones I cannot see
I carry a fumble in my legs
Weak in the knees

I carry struggle in my womb—
The one mission I can't complete
I carry my head heavy

With worries many
And failures lining up
As I lay myself on my bed

I carry all
And I carry it myself
But this flesh belongs to someone else—
Who else but the one whose weight I bear
Someone who cheers on
As I am stepped upon
By a boot so heavy
That feels but numb
"Society" that enslaved this mess
Why do you call for someone—
One who is depressed

I carry all
But it carries forward
Oh body—not fine
Can I not dream
Of you being mine?

The Hopeful/Foolish Inner Child

I look around and all I see,
Quiet and calm surrounding me.
Cries for help clash in the air,
No sighted aid in the despair.

For it has been years past long,
Since ignorance prevailed, now *the* power.
No more is there a melodious song—
The battle won; the hail storms shower.

I walk along with issues of mine,
Stone cold heart but face looks fine.
A thick metal dagger piercing my heart—
Yet, clueless kin, I fall apart.

My layers of skin touched and abused,
Body sliced open inside out.
Exposed, I lay, bleeding and bruised—
No soul left to spare—helpless, no doubt.

How do I now recognize myself?
A dreadful, poor, little victimized elf?
Maybe the tunnel retained its light—

Yet to shine, albeit un-bright.
To all the cries for help ignored,
My hand to hold, you have aboard.

Defective Fleck

I'd rather be in the dark
Than crave things bright—
Roaming in the sightless nights

Bathing in freezing colds
Not pretentious warmth;
In the cold, with my clothes on
Instead in heat—myself exposed
My mysteries, all disclosed.

This numb feels pleasure
Unlike pain—that, I won't treasure
This theatre is my bane
I grow tired of the feign.
Why must I exercise to stick?
I'm not a piece, no puzzle, no brick.

Hostility becomes me
As lovers walk the aisle, happy.
I'm no good at this show
I'd like to withdraw my role
Stay, I won't—I'd rather leave.
Debts to pay due past eve.

A humane being—odd.
Alive-ness feels a fraud.
I break bars and fly free, only—
To return in another cage built for me
It all makes me feel strange,
And I have yet to change.

I but walk on this line
Which side do I dive?
Will I reform, or will I end—
Perhaps I will never mend?

Anti-Quintessential

I painted the perfect vignette
A hot body; perfect curves
A pink sunset, black silhouette
Glimmering eyes and a sultry smirk
Smokey exhales
Cigarette in one hand
The other riding waves
Gestures crashing, talks but grand
Bold, dark shades on my lip,
Mirroring inner echoes of mine
Dreaming of kinship
My mind drowning in aged wine
Lungs soaking tar
Highs feeling gloomy
Eyes fixed to a star
Sanity going doom-y
Maybe it's time
I should quit
But isn't health a crime?
No, so be it.
When the world runs on vice
And death becomes peoplehood
Will support darken my nights
Do I face the threat of solitude

As I leave this life
Farther behind in the past
But it holds a knife
A hostage I am at heart
Yet everyone all around
So distant, outrunning
It's too late I found
To catch up, but I'm coming
The fumes entice me
Vapours calling me back
To my brain I plea
Forward I must track
Will I go on swimming
To alight the ship that sailed?
Or will I drown losing
A futile attempt derailed?

An Echo of My Likeness

I look in the mirror
At this night solitary
I look and stare—
A ghost that I can see
Pale white skin she has
Swollen periorbita, darker eyes
Deep; sorrowful

She was an eyesore, that ghost
'Twas not a mere apparition
Nothing like one would expect
Nothing like anything, she is
Stands straight, not floating translucent
I stare and glare, and she does the same.
I hate it when she looks me in the eye
I don't wish to be seen like that
I simply do not want to be seen.
Howbeit, I try peeking and she sees me again

"Stop doing that, you!"
I yell, but whisper
For I don't wish to be loud
While it's a solitary night

Why, she does nothing!
Not a blink
Just a sometimes hunch
I hate it so much

"Stop doing that, you!" command I
Why, she is doing nothing
How could she stop
If there was nothing being done

As if so elegant yet raw
She stands there, simply
Doing nothing at all, she seems rough
I can't quite put my finger on it

"You confuse me, woman," mutter I
I hate it so much
The things beyond comprehension
Failing to understand her
I see her Mona Lisa eyes, a mild hunch
And gray, fading visage
A short, stout figure
But she never speaks—
Not that she is dumb, nor wise
I hate it so much

"You look lived and spent," say I
She seems childish
She is young, also an adult
But she is never seen as a woman
Those alive see a girl
Do not question how I know her
I just do.
A collapsed discourse it is
She looks old
Someone who's lived replete
With nothing more to give
No sighs, she is tired, still
I hate it all
How she sees, how she is seen
I never want her there
She never leaves my side
I hate *her* so much
All ugly, all daft

"Go away already!" scream I
She stands there, reticent
No reaction
I hate her, for all she is.

Frustrated, I sigh—
I cannot rid myself of her
Or she of me

I think, at this moment solitary
Yet accompanied by the paranormal
And she thinks beside me

"Where are you from?" interrogate I
She does not speak
Somehow, I know the answer though
She is a ghost but does not belong
To the land of the dead
She is no acquaintance of Hades
She is from me.

Is that the cause
Of why she won't yield?
I do not wish to ponder
For she seems nothing more than a musing
Created through my vision

"It is time," declare I
Delivering a gesture
From the bits that make my face
I lift the muscles of my cheeks
I shrink my eyes
My jaw slightly clenched
And my lips stretching far and wide
I smile.

In a trice I see someone else
I see me, myself, and I
Someone I recognize
I sigh again
Not discontent; relieved

With melancholy, I smile
I miss her, *my* ghost
She seemed nice
I smile, a gesture of goodbye
Though, come morrow we shall meet again
With hair in tassels ours
We'll converse yet again
In the buzzing, sonorous silence

'Tis much like Plath's mirror
Infallible and precise
Unmoved by affection or contempt, unassuming
Yet it is rude-not, veracious
For it never lies
It devours and regurgitates
Immediate and faithful
For it is *my* mirror; a twin of Sylvia's
An honest mirror of sincere gentry
I shall see my ghost again
Each day, morning and night

I see her, my ghost
As I stopped smiling
I turn to my side, bid her goodbye
As though waving her farewell
With another encounter's promise
Turning my eyes, so is she: gone.

So goes the tale, a happenstance
An encounter betwixt me and this spectre
With Sylvia Plath's mirror, the moderator
A daily ritual – an epic
A parley within a woman
And a reflective intermediary
Each morning monotonous
And night solitary.

Hues versus Shade

Don't search for me beneath you
You won't find me there
I don't lurk around such places
Baby, I'm in the shadows
Cold, warm, and dark
I wish you bothered a little
To look sideways or up
Though I'm a shadow cast
Not that you'd see me
But I see you—crystal:
Your high and mighty
Pretentious, you stroll along
But I see you, clear as day—
Spitting that misogyny
I feel your toxic ego
Boy, what shower did you use?
I can taste the fatal musk
I see you, all days
Do you? Can you see me?
Stop searching for me
That is when you'll find me
When you stop looking
Rest up in the shade
Right there, we see us

Colours—did you paint yourself a man?
The hue's a tad bit—not you
Those baths don't suit you
Meanwhile you label me
Boring, dark and plain
Onward you try fitting in
Away, not associating with me
'Cause all colours suit you
Just not those of blood
I see you this fine evening
Colouring yourself greedy
You smirk and look at me
Seems you find me beneath you
But I breathe elsewhere
Come at me, boy
My boring, plain, dark self
Splash all that colour
And come night, I—
Devour you whole.

Rotten Blossoms

Does my vanity deceive me?
All these fancy scents, are they smoke?
Spritz from a perfume jewel—or coal?
I just wanted to be covered

Now I have to study, investigate
Styles and articulation?
Why—fabric is now canvas?
Am I ancient with my comb,
While others spark dryers?

They warned me my ancestors
They said visage is a lie
And I'll be stale, a farce
This isn't news to me
But I breathe this lie with every twitch

I play left, right, and chat in-game
Praying someone shows interest
Pitching the sale of my person
Blingy, hot and wanting?

I merge with my façade
Blurry and chaotic
Am I appealing now?
All magnetic and disguised?

Sit and sort through my tangled hair
While I lay my soul to rest
You're not needed here
Crawl in my bones, I couldn't care
In the small corner I fit myself

A grave I'm building soon
Digging deep for lowering you
My coffin adorned but cheap wood

A funeral all looks, no sensation
My eulogy who will address?

Click, Shutter, Save.

Take a photograph,
Said I to my yesterday.
Such was the urge
To tightly hold
What I lost too soon.

I think too often—
This loss of me.
Why can't we be together?
For I messed up.

Take a photograph, I didn't say.
"Hey, let's click one of us together"—
It never passed through
The crowded haste—my mind.

I think of it still.
Images I see,
But in my head, not vision—
A dull sight it is.

I should've taken a photograph.
Too hurried I was, though,
To bank all memories
That I forgot to live the moment.

Take a photograph,
Lest you lose that which you love.
I forgot to take one
Of when we were "us,"
Because I was in a rush
To create memories.

I forgot to save a memory—
And now I have nothing
To think of you by.
Just a fade in my mind
That I will lose soon...
Like I lost you.

Rose Stems on the Childhood Window

I wanted to be loved
I crave it today too
And I always got it—I guess.

(Oh, no.
I can't do this without tears
Why must I be the broken one?
How are you allowed to be okay, but I'm not?)

I am loved—the ugly kind
One where I'm the villain
But they love me "anyway"
One where I'm hurt
But I have to console them
One where I should worship them
But I detest all.

This oozing black goo
It envelops me whole
I scratch it off my skin
Flinging it away—
Piece by piece
It keeps growing, multiplying

Its venomous strands
Riding up my arms
Covering my eyes

I pick it apart, throw it
I need strength to take it off
I need to take it off to get strong
We continue this cycle
Inevitable, eternal—it seems

Change—I need, to change.
You were my gods once
My models, my icons
You glittered—I thought you diamond
But the blackness was left by coal.

How could I mis-witness it all?
Am I at fault? —No...
Then how come I'm the bad apple?
My nest I must leave
Damaged, broken—covered in soot

Maybe life outside this "abode"
Maybe someone will love me
In a way that cleanses;

A discourse that heals
Not in the way that
Buries me alive.

I loved you, and I always will
But your love hurt me
I know now.

This window will never open.
Maybe sharper vines are outside
It's time I get my own house
Grow thornless flowers
On windows that are *mine.*

Your house—no longer my home
I must brave a new world
Maybe less loving
But less cruel than yours
For these wounds may heal
But the scars will never go away.

I only hope—a strong addictive—
That beings come along
Who adore my scars
As much as they ache me.

Open and Shut

I wonder, will I make it home today?
I know that I know the way.
I can retrace my steps, alright—
One foot in front of the other, I can alight,
Use my efforts, all my might.

Seems I'm asking the wrong question.
Do I wish to make it home? —The right suggestion.
Since it takes a lot more than tying up a shoelace,
You realise that yet, you've only scratched the surface.

I can dive deeper than ever—
To unfold that which is hidden,
Making my way through open doors once forbidden.

I fear more than I wonder, though,
Will I like what I see,
Stepping on water, as doors open to the sea?
What if I decide to dive through,
Swimming in deeper and deeper blue?

Now that I'm under these waters,
I forget—do I swim for the surface or the bottom?
Maybe these doors were closed for issues,
Forbidden for reasons some—and dues.

The cold bothers the water, not me.
Walking on thin ice—never reassuring.
Ice break may not be a good thing;
After all, scratching the frozen liquid
Was ample enough for kin.

I keep my wonders stored within me,
Frozen cold in the attic of my mind.
As I tie a shoelace—a small fee—
And I retrace those steps I wished not to find.

Someday, I promise to myself,
I'll open that cold, dark box on the shelf,
And reignite stark fires of my blackening curiosity—
Finally uniting, long awaited,
With Oblivion, *my* deity.

Lingering Drowse

Wishes I only have but one
I want to sail in a sea—
Nay, an ocean of good dreams

Float above calm waters
As I drift away in peace...

But I can't commandeer this boat
I just broke both my oars
Am I stuck on land amid a storm,
With all its chaos unveiling?

I want to close my eyes
Repair my core for the night
But I force them awake—
The masts holding my lids and lashes
My mind refuses to part away
From this—the waking world
I can't live without this horror, it would seem

I force myself wide awake
While my body cries for slumber
I must fight daylight for recompense,
For the life it took from me

A day lived for but without me
As I serve printed paper,
Created joy eluding me.

This dark soiree must last
As a delirious me coerces
Elation for one blink
Before I sail away
Amongst unsettling waves
To those horrors of beyond

Because I need to get up,
Tired again—my eyes gloomy
Rewind, repeat and play
Till my soul fast forwards
And boat lands ashore again—
My life having fled by me.

A Convalescent Pill Caddy

Silent I stayed for so long
In quiet anguish my life advanced
To write my own song
Didn't think I'd get a chance

Sought solace in ill health
Drowning in hand-picked cocktails
Cribbing about the cards dealt
Did nothing but cry and wail

Combining that with drags and puffs
Thought it a brilliant suggestion
Coughs, vomit, body losing trust
Why do I need help? —I'm fine, I mention

Shame darkens my room
Friends I have only some
Welcome anxiety, depression, doom
We all share this space—numb

An army outside
Trying to break this bond
While I cower and hide
They wave their magic wand

I step out holding my friends' hands
Everything stale and pale
A new magic the soldiers land
Medicine—the wizardry—prevails

The soldiers were disguised
My true companions they were
Cloaked as enemies ill-advised
Carried aid, support—but it's all a blur

I lug my feet into the clinic
Rage and terror in my bones
Apprehensive; a total cynic
Entering the room, my mind drones

I am ready with my sword and shield
Anticipating attack; a warrior
But I am met with melody
I let down my guard and barriers

A tiny obelisk I am prescribed
"Are you sure this is okay?"
"Yes," he says—with care imbibed
Here it goes, I wash it down everyday

Something shifts to a new tune
Trees greener and flowers pinker
The sky seems a deeper blue
My eyes, unlike before, glimmer

Have I gone bonkers, finally?
My friends now distant than before
Maybe this is happy?
Perhaps the tiny thing opened a new door

Exposed I see that
My "friends" were dragging me
Now I have leashes at last
Not cured but on a beat

I'm a pill popper
Or so they say
But life is now technicolour
Instead of greys.

Intimate Leaves

Every day my feet grope marble
But today—not.
I don't untie my shoelaces but
I remove my shoes, and my socks
And I let my mother hold me.

She blows a relieving wind
Cooled by the green woods,
My skin basking in
The suspended rays of sun.

The grass is not all green
But fresh—as is the dirt.
A turn stumbles in my heart
Change is what I feel—
My mood, soul, mind, and thoughts
All calming me.

It hits like a dose,
Shooting up a vaccine
Against the cancer of dull
And rotting feels.

I breathe—long and slow
Blossoming furry bonds.
I lay with my shadow,
Freeing from myself.

Alas, I have to leave—
Since my mother is not my home
But a bare picnic hour.

Wearing my shoes, I pick myself up
Turning away from her consoling grace.
Return I must, for my job awaits.

I am now mechanical—
No longer alive, again.
Left the fresh behind,
Right back to the grind.

Sonder, I lie, begging
As I drift away to grayscale bedding
Turning to wax—
And I lose my form
More than a feeling
That's bent out of shape.

But I remembered to take pictures,
To rewind and reminisce.

I'll work hard, time and tide.
Another appointment I have made—
My ma I will visit, and—
In love we'll hold each other.

A Dreamscape Olive Branch

I want to find my home in the woods
But the darker mists scare me
Even though the leaves hide sunlight,
Moonlit ghosts appear bright

What if there are wolves at night
Howling at the big, glowing ball in the sky?
Maybe someone's playing yo-yo
With a luminescent sphere,
And the light switch turned off,
Attracting owls and moths alike

What if I am a prey in waiting,
About to be ravaged
By rage, wreck, and despair?
Do the wolves see me an enemy
Or do they see a reflection?
None of these a safety net
If I whisk past their turf

Oh, oh! Maybe I'll invite the wolves
For a tea party and potluck
They'll bite down the meat
While I snack on fruits and berries

And the fireflies will illuminate my tiny house—
Larger than my life
And accommodating to all
Cave-like holes, burrows and cushions
They can take their pick
Whatever's comfy and appealing
We can run around chasing each other
Our feet's friction sparking joy

I'll plan to befriend the hostile beasts
By feeding them my best recipes
For we starve together,
Thirsty for the same caring waters
We might misunderstand one another—
Both hunters, and hunted—
Though we carry no ill will

I'll add a dash of regret
Two cups of promises and apologies
Forgiveness a bowl-full,
All stirred together
I hope they feast 'fore their verdict—
May they let me in, or kill me swiftly—
Neither scented with doom
But both rhyming with harmony

Escape might be my medicine
From buildings or being
The green trail a remedy
My future whispering peace

I don't belong in this beige city
Where neighbours poach and bridges burn
I don't want this modernity
I yearn the dew on leaves
And the melody of brown roots

I'm too tired to build an abode
Just want to find one already made
Germinated, ready for my presence
Equipped with cozy familiarity

Forest life awaiting
And love from the trees—
Always there, a quiet reverie,
Standing tall and supportive

I want to trot away free
I must stretch my limbs
Disembark and run like an animal
It's a lengthy, narrow way—
The destination awoken early

Unlike the race track weary,
I paced along with breath each
Was alone together with many
But selected the other path

I was born to parents an orphan
Now I am embraced as their own
By all in my tender home.

Dire Miracles

What happens to this journey of mine?
Forged by the fires of my soul that shine
Blind have I become to this ritual crime
Forgotten through the haze of giving a dime

Spacing out from my whole world
Passive in participation, thoughts unfurled
Why am I not being penalized
Those fires destroying while my conscience hides

Is it good to know or better to not?
They kill me alive—the answers I once sought
Gone is the age of curious, a mark
Dead the light of knowledge, lost in the dark.

Can I clear and clean up this debris
Are help and aid the necessity?
A momentous repair—can we make it happen?
Reclaim the conscious, let's strap in.

Has the cold around me made me warm?
Chasing nothing but air in the storm
Accomplices are many, friends though none
Is this realized task only *my* burden?

A lonesome destination I had set
Together we could build, not just abet
What happens to this journey of mine?
Oh, Jesus! Turn this water to wine.

Author's Stitches

My body is a story.
The dead, damaged, and live cells
Shedding, repairing, renewing
They all pass through time
And through their own lives.

The flesh sequences the plot
And flipping calendars, the storyline
Set in Industry 4.0, the 21st century
On an almost-sphere of dust and water
A suburban area, rich-ish working family
A proletariat mindset, revering hard work!

My body is a story, my mind the protagonist.
The characters, the cast, it all keeps changing
Come and go, as life permits.
The antagonist eludes me,
Maybe life is my enemy.

This is an unusual story
The theme is "alive"
In a manner of speaking
The tone in plural descriptions
I misunderstood my own story.

You see, it is mine
But not written in my style
Maybe the red thread of fate
Or the randomness of an indifferent cosmos
It's written in peculiar fonts
Bizarre moments, eerie silences
Weird sounds and strange sights.

You may choose not to believe me
But I carry always proof:
Clothes that used to fit me
Worn out shoes and stained bedsheets
Scratched mirrors, bruises and paper cuts
I have an academic degree in a name—
I can't connect to any longer.
Yellowing books that remain unopened
Their spines uncracked, begging to be read
Shortened pencils and vanishing erasers
Eye bags and fine lines
Stretch marks and scars.

Yes, I have scars so many
Perhaps I have become obsolete
Needing a replacement
For the remaining sand in my life-glass
I bathe in the spotlight no more
Maybe I never did

My enemy—but maybe a *neutral* entity—
Life has overtaken me
Leaving me behind
With baggage heavy and frail organs
To play catch-up and run all time.

Exposition you get none.
After all, I never did.
Turning days like pages
Sifting through climaxes
Culminating aches, smiles, and pains.

But resolved isn't this story
My body has more to write.
Blank pages await
Scar-less skin is fresh
Longing for newer wounds
As old ones infect or heal

I guess I'll choose my wounds
From this day forward
And maybe beg Life for
A race slower than the stacking nights
At this minute a work-in-progress.

When I die, when my story nears closure
Use my ashes to plant a tree
So I'll have somewhere to dwell
I might haunt a tourist or two
On random evening whims
And my body will rest
When Life decides.
The story will meet a conclusion
All tensions will resolve
Networks will disconnect
And I will dissolve into the bookshelf.

Going

Every step I take,
All appears fake.
One step forward,
To steps backward.
Is that what's said?
You make it—and die in your bed?

I'm only human,
And look at what I've done—
Consumed with what could be,
Forgotten what would be.
Is this to be my legacy?
Ruins and ravages in memory?

A traveller at heart,
No distinct destination apart.
Wandering with a hopeless soul,
Swinging to the melody—no goal.
Do I sit back and take a breath?
Or do I keep going until my death?

Look at me going on and on—
Too many questions asked at dawn.
So much noise from all around...

I guess I'll make my own sound:
A new truth that I have found,
As I lay newborn on nature's ground.

Sing With Me

I still have music in me
I rage, I deceive, and I grieve
But I'm not done—not yet
Eons more to go, my end I haven't met
Many impossibles I need to conquer
To create beauty, magic, and sonder

I still have music in me
My last song not in the right key
But I sang then, as I sing now
My magnum opus awaits—then I'll take a bow
My struggle is the composition
I'm tuning it to my rendition
Not all albums fair the same
I might not go down in fame

I still have music in me
Rehearsals and microphones reign in tyranny
My tones are not landing dulcet
Practice the harmonies—I won't forget
Headset on, I lay on dewy grass
Humming to melodies that I will surpass
The right coach I shall find
My training is destined, designed

I still have music in me
I'll sing to an audience, free
Standing ovations and crowd noise
Encores will be requested—twice
It'll be the best performance ever
In peace I will be, but rest—never

So close your eyes and listen
Hear my symphony and watch me glisten
I will shatter sealed windows and doors—
Repair, heal, and reveal your souls.

I still have music left in me
And my voice will carry thee.

www.ingramcontent.com/pod-product-compliance
Lightning Source LLC
LaVergne TN
LVHW021240200726
843509LV00012B/1544